PLACE HOLDER FOR OUTSIDE COVER PAGE

-DISCARD ONCE PRINTED-

Contact Us!

Dr. Nicki Newton

Email: gigglenook@gmail.com

Website: www.drnicki123.com

Blog: guidedmath.wordpress.com

Also by Dr. Nicki Newton

Guided Math in Action: Building Math Proficiency
Problem Solving With Math Models: Grade K
Problem Solving With Math Models: Grade 2
Problem Solving With Math Models: Grade 3
Problem Solving With Math Models: Grade 4
Problem Solving With Math Models: Grade 5

PROBLEM SOLVING™

WITH MATH MODELS

FIRST GRADE

DR. NICKI NEWTON

Gigglenook Publication
P.O. Box 110134
Trumbull CT 06611
Email: gigglenook@gmail.com
Website: www.drnicki123.com
Produced by GiggleNook Publications
Thank you to the entire Production

Chief Operating Officer: Dr. Nicki Newton
Publisher: Gigglenook Publication
Cover Design: This Way Up Productions
Text Design and Composition: Bonnie Harrison-Jones

Printed in the United States of America
ISBN-13: 978-1493521784
ISBN-10: 1493521780
Volume 1: December 2012

Dedicated to Mom and Pops, Always

TABLE OF CONTENTS

FOREWORD

Story problems can be great! Story problems are the stuff life is made of. If we can make connections for children between their daily lives and the problems we pose and solve in school, we will have much more success. We need to provide scaffolds into the process.

The New Math Common Core (2010) places a big emphasis on problem solving. The first mathematical practice mentioned states that students should "Make sense of problems and persevere in solving them." It goes on to describe this by stating that mathematically proficient students should be able to explain a problem and find ways to enter into it. According to the New Math Common Core students should be able to solve problems with objects, drawings and equations. In this book, students will practice word problems aligned to the standards by using the CCSS designated math models.

The Math Common Core, actually adopted the framework for story problems, created by Carpenter, Fennema, Franke, Levi & Empson, 1999; Peterson, Fennema & Carpenter (1989). The research says that the more teachers understand these types of problems and teach them to their students, the better students understand the problems and are able to solve them. Furthermore, the research makes the case that the KEY WORD METHOD should be avoided! Students should learn to understand the problem types and what they are actually discussing rather than "key word" tricks. The thing about key words is that they only work with really simplistic problems and so as students do more sophisticated work with word problems, the key words do not serve them well. They may actually lead them in the wrong direction, often encouraging the wrong operation. For example, given this problem: *John has 2 apples. Kate has 3 more than he does. How many do they have altogether?* Many students just add 2 and 3 instead of unpacking the problem. Another example, given this problem: *Sue has 10 marbles. She has 2 times as many marbles as Lucy. How many marbles does Lucy have?*

Often times, students just multiply because they see the word *times*, instead of really reading and understanding the problem.

This book is about giving students a repertoire of tools, models and strategies to help them think about, understand and solve word problems. We want to scaffold reasoning opportunities from the concrete (using objects) to the pictorial (pictures and drawings) and, finally, to the abstract (writing equations).

DR. NICKI NEWTON

ACKNOWLEDGEMENTS

I would like to thank many people for their support, expertise, guidance, and encouragement during this project. First of all I would like to thank God, without him this would not be possible. Second, I would like to thank my mom, pa, big mom, and granddaddy. Third, I would like to thank my family for all their love and support, especially my Tia that calls me every day and asks me "What have you accomplished today?" Next, I would like to thank all of my friends that support me all the time. This book series would not have been possible without the continual support of all of them. Finally, I would like to thank everyone that has helped me write this book. There have been many people from the Gigglenook Team that have worked on this project. Thank you to all of you for your continual support.

INTRODUCTION TO THE TYPES OF PROBLEMS

Grade Specific Problem Solving Expectations

The CCSS is very specific about what students should be able to do in terms of solving word problems by grade levels. In pre-k students should be exposed to addition and subtraction story problem situations with numbers through 5. By kindergarten they should work with these types of problems as well as part/part whole problems through 10. But, in first grade there is a big leap. The standards say that the children will be able to work with the above-mentioned three types as well as comparison problems with unknowns in all positions with a symbol for the unknown to represent the problem through 20. They should also be able to solve word problems with three numbers adding up to 20. By second grade, they have to do the same thing with all problem types, including the harder comparison problems but through 100.

Adding to Problems

Adding to problems are all about adding. There are three types. The first type is adding to/ putting together problems where the result is unknown. For example: *Jenny had 5 marbles. John gave her 3 more. How many marbles does Jenny have altogether now?* In this problem the result is unknown. Teachers tend to tell these types of problems. They are basic and straight forward. The teacher should start with concrete items and then proceed to drawing out the story and then diagramming the story and finally putting the equations to the story. This is the easiest type of story to solve.

The second kind of Adding to Problem is a Change Unknown problem. For example: *Jenny had 5 marbles. John gave her some more. Now she has 8 marbles. How many marbles did John give her?* In this type of problem, the students are looking for the change. They know the start and they know the end but they don't know the change. So, students have to put down the start and then count up to how many. Students could also start with 8 marbles and take away the original 5 to see how many more were added to make 8. This problem type is introduced in 1st grade.

The third type of Adding to Problem is a Start Unknown problem. For example: *Jenny had some marbles. John gave her 3 more. Now she has 8 marbles. How many marbles did Jenny have in the beginning?* In this type of problem, the students are looking for the start. This is the hardest type of Adding to Problem to solve. This takes a great deal of modeling. Although 1st graders may be exposed to this problem type, they are not expected to have full mastery of it.

Taking From Problems

Taking From problems are all about subtracting. There are three types. The first type is taking from problems where the result is unknown. For example: *Jenny had 5 marbles. She gave John 3. How many marbles does Jenny have left?* In this problem the result is unknown. Teachers tend to tell these types of problems. They are basic and straight forward. The teacher should start with concrete items and then proceed to drawing out the story and then diagramming the story and finally putting the equations to the story.

The second kind of Taking from problem is the Change Unknown problem. For example: *Jenny had 10 marbles. She gave John some. Now she has 8 marbles left. How many marbles did she give to John?* In this type of problem, the students are looking for the change. They know the start and they know the end but they don't know the change. So, students could put down the start and then count up to how many. Students could also start with 10 marbles and take away some until they have 8 left. They would count to see how many they had to take away to remain with 8. This problem type is introduced in 1st grade.

The third type of Taking from Problem is a Start Unknown problem. For example: *Jenny had some marbles. She gave John 3. Now she has 7 marbles left. How many marbles did Jenny have to start with?* In this type of problem, the students are looking for the start. This is the hardest type of Taking from Problem to solve. This takes a great deal of modeling. You can use ten frames to show this. One strategy is to have the students put down the seven Jenny has left and count up three to see how many there are in total.

Although 1st grade students might be introduced to these problems, they are not expected to master them until 2nd grade.

Part Part Whole Problems

A Part Part Whole problem is a problem that discusses the two parts and the whole. There are three types of Part Part Whole Problems. The first type is called Whole Unknown. For example: *Susie has some marbles. Five are red and five are blue. How many marbles does she have altogether?* We know both parts and the task is to figure out the whole.

The second kind of problem is called Both Addends Unknown. For example: *Susie has 5 marbles. Some are green and some are blue. How many marbles could she have of each?* We have to figure out all of the possible combinations. It is important to specify whether or not all of the marbles are used or not.

The third kind of problem is called Part Unknown. For example, *Susie has 10 marbles. Seven are red. The rest are blue. How many are blue?* In this type of problem, we are given the whole and one of the parts. The task is to figure out the other part. The New Common Core refers to this type of problem as a Taking Apart Problem. This problem type is introduced in 1st grade.

Comparing Stories – All of these problems are introduced in 1st grade for the first time.

Comparing Stories are the most difficult types of stories to tell. There are three types of comparison stories. The first type of comparing story is where two different things are being compared. For example, *Susie had ten lollipops and Kayla had eight. How many more lollipops did Susie have than Kayla?*

The second type of comparing story is where the Bigger Part is Unknown. In this type of story, we are looking for the bigger amount. For example, *Susie had 4 candies. Maya had 3 more than her. How many candies did Maya have?* Here, we know what Susie had, and then in comparison, Maya had 3 more. The task is to find the bigger part.

The third type of comparing story is to find the smaller part. This is considered the hardest type of addition/subtraction story to solve. For example, *Jaya has 7 candies. She has 3 more than Marcos. How many does Marcos have?* In this type of story we know what Jaya has and we know that she has 3 more than Marcos. We are looking for the smaller amount. We only know about what Marcos has in comparison to what Jaya has. The task is to use the information given to find the smaller part.

INTRODUCING THE MODELS FOR THINKING

There are several great tools to use for solving number stories. In this book students will use different tools to think about the word problems. They will use Number Frames, Number Grids, Number Bonds, Drawings, Number lines and Tables.

Number Frames

Number frames provide a visual scaffold for children to understand word problems. There are 3 different types of number frames - The Five Frame, the Ten Frame, and the Double Ten Frame. Five is the first anchor number so we should always start with Five Frames, although few math programs do. Ten is foundational and many math programs do use this frame. Finally, the Double Ten Frame helps to increase the range of number in word problems. Number frames are visual scaffolds that help students to see what they are doing and think about the numbers in different ways.

FIVE FRAME

TEN FRAME

Drawings

The CCSS (2010) states that all students should know how to model their thinking with a drawing. It emphasizes that students should understand how to do a sketch rather than a detailed drawing. For example: *Susie had 2 stickers. Her cousin gave her 3 more. How many does she have altogether?*

The Number Line

The Number Line is another important model that is emphasized throughout the CCSS (2010). For example: *Sue had 8 stickers. John gave her 2 more. How many does she have now?*

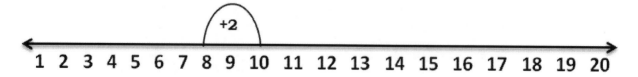

Problem Solving with Math Models© 2012

The Number Bond

The Number Bond is a model that helps children to focus on the meaning of the quantity. It requires that children think about the numbers they are using and have the ability to compose and decompose them. For example: *Sue has 10 apples. John gave her 2 more. How many does she have now?*

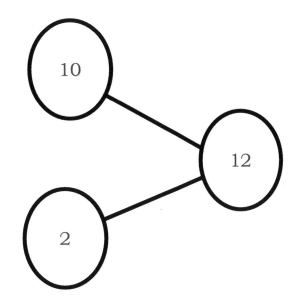

Another example: *Sue had 10 apples. She gave 2 to John. How many does she have now?*

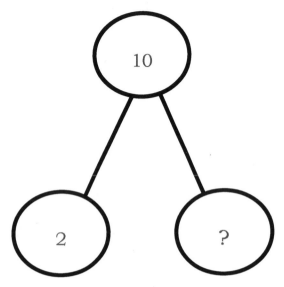

Tables

When solving Both Addend Unknown problems, students should be encouraged to model their thinking with drawings and tables. For example: *John had 5 marbles. Some were red and some were blue. If he had some of each, how many could he have had?*

MARBLES	
Red	**Blue**
4	1
3	2
2	3
1	4

Equations

The CCSSM (2010) states that 1st graders need to know how to write an equation with a symbol for the unknown. Teachers should use a variety of symbols with the students such as question marks, empty boxes, letters and hearts. In this book we will use a question mark for the unknown for consistency. For example: *Sue had 5 stickers. Her mother gave her some more. Now, she has 10. How many did her mother give her?   5 + ? = 10.*

TEACHER TIPS:

- When you introduce the problem, be sure to tell the students what type of problem it is.

- Remember that you can take the same problem and rework it in different ways throughout the week.

- Work on a problem type until the students are proficient at recognizing and solving that problem type. Also give them opportunities to write and tell that specific problem type.

- Be sure to contextualize the problems in the students' everyday lives. Using the problems in the book as models, substitute the students' names and their everyday things.

- Be sure to provide tons of guided practice. Solve problems together as a class, with partners and in groups. Individual practice should come after the students have had plenty of opportunities to work together and comprehend and understand what they are doing.

- Emphasize that there is no one correct way to solve a problem but that there is usually only one correct answer.

- Encourage students to always show their work.

CHAPTER 1
ADD TO RESULT UNKNOWN PROBLEMS

These types of problems are the easiest types of addition problems. In these problems students are looking for what happened at the end of the story. We know what we started with and what we added to that part. We are trying to find out how many we have altogether now.

PROBLEM	John had 10 marbles. Henry gave him 7 more. How many does he have now?
MODEL	+7 ⌢ ←— 10 ———————— 17 —→
EQUATION	$10 + 7 = ?$ $10 + 7 = 17$

PROBLEM	Imani had 5 stickers. Her mother gave her 5 more. How many does she have altogether now?
MODEL	5 — 5 — ?
EQUATION	$5 + 5 = ?$ $5 + 5 = 10$

Problem Solving with Math Models© 2012

ADD TO RESULT UNKNOWN

1. Lili has 4 marbles. Dana gave her 1 more. How many marbles does Lili have now?

Way#1: Solve with a five frame

Way#2: Model with a number line

1 2 3 4 5 6 7 8 9 10 11 12 13 14 15 16 17 18 19 20

Way#3: Write a number sentence with a symbol for the part you don't know

_____ + _____ = _____

ADD TO RESULT UNKNOWN

2. Brett has 3 baseballs. Pete gave him 2 more. How many baseballs does Brett have now?

Way#1: Solve with a five frame

Way#2: Model with a number line

1 2 3 4 5 6 7 8 9 10 11 12 13 14 15 16 17 18 19 20

Way#3: Write a number sentence with a symbol for the part you don't know

_____+_____ = _____

ADD TO RESULT UNKNOWN

3. Lisa picked 5 flowers on Monday. Then she did not pick anymore on Tuesday. How many does she have now?

Way#1: Model with a number bond

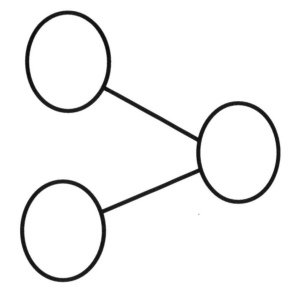

Way#2: Model with a number line

1 2 3 4 5 6 7 8 9 10 11 12 13 14 15 16 17 18 19 20

Way#3: Write a number sentence with a symbol for the part you don't know

_____ + _____ = _____

ADD TO RESULT UNKNOWN

4. Andy has 3 rocks in his collection. Danny gave him 3 more. How many does Andy have now?

Way#1: Model with a drawing

Way#2: Model with a number line

$$1 \quad 2 \quad 3 \quad 4 \quad 5 \quad 6 \quad 7 \quad 8 \quad 9 \quad 10 \quad 11 \quad 12 \quad 13 \quad 14 \quad 15 \quad 16 \quad 17 \quad 18 \quad 19 \quad 20$$

Way#3: Write a number sentence with a symbol for the part you don't know

_____+_____ = _____

            Problem Solving with Math Models© 2012

ADD TO RESULT UNKNOWN

5. John had 5 action figures. Tom gave him 5 more. How many action figures does John have now?

Way#1: Solve with a ten frame

Way#2: Model with a number line

1 2 3 4 5 6 7 8 9 10 11 12 13 14 15 16 17 18 19 20

Way#3: Write a number sentence with a symbol for the part you don't know

_____ + _____ = _____

ADD TO RESULT UNKNOWN

6. Justine had 7 pennies. Her sister gave her 3 more. How many pennies does Justine have now?

Way#1: Solve with a ten frame

Way#2: Model with a number line

1 2 3 4 5 6 7 8 9 10 11 12 13 14 15 16 17 18 19 20

Way#3: Write a number sentence with a symbol for the part you don't know

_____ + _____ = _____

ADD TO RESULT UNKNOWN

7. The bakery made 12 lemon cupcakes. Then they made 8 more cupcakes. How many did they make altogether?

Way#1: Solve with a double ten frame.

Way#2: Model with a number line

$$\xleftarrow{\hspace{1cm}} 1\ 2\ 3\ 4\ 5\ 6\ 7\ 8\ 9\ 10\ 11\ 12\ 13\ 14\ 15\ 16\ 17\ 18\ 19\ 20 \xrightarrow{\hspace{1cm}}$$

Way#3: Write a number sentence with a symbol for the part you don't know

_____ + _____ = _____

ADD TO RESULT UNKNOWN

8. Farmer John picked 4 apples, 4 oranges and 4 peaches from his trees. How many fruits did he pick altogether?

Way#1: Solve with a double ten frame.

Way#2: Model with a number line

1 2 3 4 5 6 7 8 9 10 11 12 13 14 15 16 17 18 19 20

Way#3: Write a number sentence with a symbol for the part you don't know

_____ + _____ = _____

CHAPTER 1 QUIZ:
ADD TO RESULT UNKNOWN

Solve with a model:

1. Frank had 2 marbles. His brother gave him 5 more. How many does he have now?

2. Maria had 5 rings. She got 9 more for her birthday. How many rings does she have now?

3. Daniel had 7 action figures. He bought 7 more. How many does he have now?

4. Sue made 2 pink bracelets. Then she made 3 green bracelets and 4 orange ones. How many bracelets did she make altogether?

CHAPTER 2
ADD TO CHANGE UNKNOWN PROBLEMS

In these problems students are looking for what happened in the middle of the story. In this type of story we know what happened at the beginning but then some change happened and now we have more than we started with at the end. We are trying to find out how many things were added in the middle of the story.

PROBLEM	John had 5 marbles. His mother gave him some more. Now he has 12. How many did his mother give him?
MODEL	
EQUATION	5 + ? = 12 5 + 7 = 12

PROBLEM	May had 7 stickers. Her mother gave her some more. Now, she has 14 stickers. How many did her mother give her?
MODEL	
EQUATION	7 + ? = 14 7 + 7 = 14

ADD TO CHANGE UNKNOWN

1. Chung has 2 toy airplanes. Matt gave him some more. Now he has 4 toy airplanes. How many airplanes did Matt give him?

Way#1: Solve with a ten frame

Way#2: Model with a number line

1 2 3 4 5 6 7 8 9 10 11 12 13 14 15 16 17 18 19 20

Way#3: Write a number sentence with a symbol for the part you don't know

_____ + _____ = _____

ADD TO CHANGE UNKNOWN

2. Judy had 8 cookies. Lisa gave her some more cookies. Now Judy has 10 cookies. How many cookies did Lisa give her?

Way#1: Solve with a ten frame

Way#2: Model with a number line

$$\longleftarrow \overline{} \longrightarrow$$

1 2 3 4 5 6 7 8 9 10 11 12 13 14 15 16 17 18 19 20

Way#3: Write a number sentence with a symbol for the part you don't know

_____ + _____ = _____

ADD TO CHANGE UNKNOWN

3.   John had 8 toy soldiers. Ellen gave him some more. Now he has 15. How many toy soldiers did Ellen give him?

Way#1: Solve with a double ten frame.

Way#2: Model with a number line

1 2 3 4 5 6 7 8 9 10 11 12 13 14 15 16 17 18 19 20

Way#3: Write a number sentence with a symbol for the part you don't know

_____ + _____ = _____

ADD TO CHANGE UNKNOWN

4. David had 5 toy cars. Steve gave him some more. Now he has 11 toy cars. How many toy cars did Steve give him?

Way#1: Solve with a drawing

Way#2: Model with a number line

1 2 3 4 5 6 7 8 9 10 11 12 13 14 15 16 17 18 19 20

Way#3: Write a number sentence with a symbol for the part you don't know

_____ + _____ = _____

ADD TO CHANGE UNKNOWN

5. Gary had 7 stuffed animals. He got some more for his birthday. Now he has 14 stuffed animals. How many stuffed animals did he get for his birthday?

Way#1: Model with a number bond

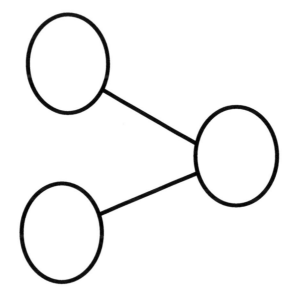

Way#2: Model with a number line

1 2 3 4 5 6 7 8 9 10 11 12 13 14 15 16 17 18 19 20

Way#3: Write a number sentence with a symbol for the part you don't know

_____ + _____ = _____

Problem Solving with Math Models© 2012

ADD TO CHANGE UNKNOWN

6. Luke had 10 seashells. His brother gave him some more. Now he has 15. How many seashells did his brother give him?

Way#1: Solve with a drawing

Way#2: Model with a number line

$$\longleftarrow\!\!\!\!\!\xrightarrow{\ 1\ \ 2\ \ 3\ \ 4\ \ 5\ \ 6\ \ 7\ \ 8\ \ 9\ \ 10\ \ 11\ \ 12\ \ 13\ \ 14\ \ 15\ \ 16\ \ 17\ \ 18\ \ 19\ \ 20\ }$$

Way#3: Write a number sentence with a symbol for the part you don't know

_____ + _____ = _____

ADD TO CHANGE UNKNOWN

7. There were 7 cookies in the jar. Grandma Betsy put some more in the jar and now there are 12 cookies. How many cookies did she put in the jar?

Way#1: Solve with a double ten frame.

Way#2: Model with a number line

1 2 3 4 5 6 7 8 9 10 11 12 13 14 15 16 17 18 19 20

Way#3: Write a number sentence with a symbol for the part you don't know

_____ + _____ = _____

Problem Solving with Math Models© 2012

ADD TO CHANGE UNKNOWN

8. The toy store had 12 action figures. They got another shipment and now they have 20 action figures. How many action figures did they get?

Way#1: Solve with a double ten frame.

Way#2: Model with a number line

1 2 3 4 5 6 7 8 9 10 11 12 13 14 15 16 17 18 19 20

Way#3: Write a number sentence with a symbol for the part you don't know

_____ + _____ = _____

CHAPTER 2 QUIZ:
ADD TO CHANGE UNKNOWN PROBLEMS

Solve with a model:

1. Sally had 6 stickers and Judy gave her some more. Now she has 10 stickers. How many did Judy give her?

2. Carol had 7 marbles. Tim gave her some more. Now she has 12 marbles. How many did Tim give her?

3.   The bakery baked 12 cookies in the morning. In the afternoon, they baked some more. Now they have 20 cookies.   How many cookies did they bake in the afternoon?

4.   The pizza shop made 9 mini-pizzas. Then they made some more. Now they have 18 mini-pizzas. How many more pizzas did they make?

Unit 1 Test:
Addition Problems

Solve with a model:

1. Mary had 1 dress. For her birthday, she got 2 more. How many dresses does she have now?

2. Ricky had 2 basketballs. He bought 5 more. His brother gave him 4 more. How many basketballs does he have now?

Problem Solving with Math Models© 2012

3. The bakery made 5 pies in the morning and some more in the afternoon. Now they have 20 pies. How many did they make in the afternoon?

4. Carla had 16 seashells. Tim gave her some more. Now she has 17. How many did Tim give her?

CHAPTER 1
TAKE FROM RESULT UNKNOWN PROBLEMS

In these problems students are looking for what happened in the end of the story. In this type of story we know what happened at the beginning and also what change occurred. We are trying to find out how many things remained after some things were taken away.

PROBLEM	Ray had 10 apples. He gave 5 away. How many does he have left?
MODEL	
EQUATION	$10 - ? = 5$ $10 - 5 = 5$

PROBLEM	Maria had 10 stickers. She gave 4 to her sister. How many does she have left?
MODEL	
EQUATION	$10 - 4 = ?$ $10 - 4 = 6$

TAKE FROM RESULT UNKNOWN

1. Farmer Lee picked 5 apples from the apple tree. She ate 2 apples. How many apples does she have left?

Way#1: Solve with a five frame

Way#2: Model with a number line

Way#3: Write a number sentence with a symbol for the part you don't know

_____ - _____ = _____

TAKE FROM RESULT UNKNOWN

2. Candy had 10 stickers. She gave 5 to Heather. How many stickers does she have left?

Way#1: Solve with a ten frame

Way#2: Model with a number line

1 2 3 4 5 6 7 8 9 10 11 12 13 14 15 16 17 18 19 20

Way#3: Write a number sentence with a symbol for the part you don't know

_____ - _____ = _____

TAKE FROM RESULT UNKNOWN

3. Brett had 12 marbles. He gave 6 marbles to John. How many marbles does he have now?

Way#1: Solve with a double ten frame.

Way#2: Model with a number line

← 1 2 3 4 5 6 7 8 9 10 11 12 13 14 15 16 17 18 19 20 →

Way#3: Write a number sentence with a symbol for the part you don't know

_____ - _____ = _____

TAKE FROM RESULT UNKNOWN

4. Tammy had 10 butterfly stamps. She used 4 stamps. How many stamps does she have left?

Way#1: Model with a number bond

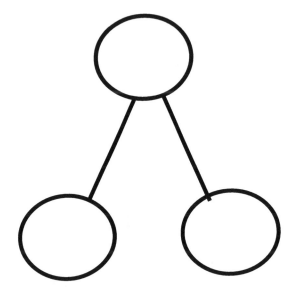

Way#2: Model with a number line

1 2 3 4 5 6 7 8 9 10 11 12 13 14 15 16 17 18 19 20

Way#3: Write a number sentence with a symbol for the part you don't know

_____ - _____ = _____

Take From Result Unknown

5. Benny had 7 books. He read 5. How many books does he have left to read?

Way#1: Solve with a drawing

Way#2: Model with a number line

$$\xleftarrow{\hspace{0.5em}} 1 \quad 2 \quad 3 \quad 4 \quad 5 \quad 6 \quad 7 \quad 8 \quad 9 \quad 10 \quad 11 \quad 12 \quad 13 \quad 14 \quad 15 \quad 16 \quad 17 \quad 18 \quad 19 \quad 20 \xrightarrow{\hspace{0.5em}}$$

Way#3: Write a number sentence with a symbol for the part you don't know

_____ - _____ = _____

Take from Result Unknown

6. Becky had 9 stickers. She gave 2 stickers to her sister. How many stickers does she have now?

Way#1: Solve with a ten frame

Way#2: Model with a number line

$$\longleftrightarrow$$
1 2 3 4 5 6 7 8 9 10 11 12 13 14 15 16 17 18 19 20

Way#3: Write a number sentence with a symbol for the part you don't know

_____ - _____ = _____

TAKE FROM RESULT UNKNOWN

7. Tim had 18 baseballs. He gave away 8 of them. How many does he have left?

Way#1: Model with a number bond

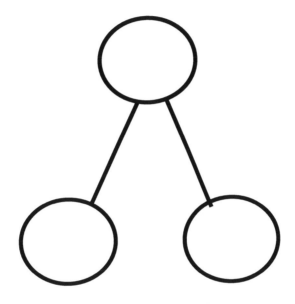

Way#2: Model with a number line

1 2 3 4 5 6 7 8 9 10 11 12 13 14 15 16 17 18 19 20

Way#3: Write a number sentence with a symbol for the part you don't know

_____ - _____ = _____

TAKE FROM RESULT UNKNOWN

8. Farmer Dan had 15 peaches. He sold 8 of them at the market. How many peaches does he have left?

Way#1: Solve with a drawing

Way#2: Model with a number line

← 1 2 3 4 5 6 7 8 9 10 11 12 13 14 15 16 17 18 19 20 →

Way#3: Write a number sentence with a symbol for the part you don't know

_____ - _____ = _____

CHAPTER 1 QUIZ:
TAKE FROM RESULT UNKNOWN PROBLEMS

Solve with a model:

1. Manny had 16 kittens. He gave 8 to his friend. How many does he have now?

2. Maria had 10 seashells. She gave 5 away. How many does she have left?

3.   Paul had 18 toy cars.   He gave 4 away.   How many does he have left?

4.   The bakery made 17 brownies.   They sold 8.   How many cookies do they have left?

Problem Solving with Math Models© 2012

CHAPTER 2
TAKE FROM CHANGE UNKNOWN PROBLEMS

In these problems students are looking for what happened in the middle of the story. In this type of story we know what happened at the beginning but then some change happened and now we have less than we started with by the end of the story. We are trying to find out how many things were taken away in the middle of the story.

PROBLEM	John had 15 marbles. He gave some to his cousin. Now he has 12 left. How many did he give to his cousin?
MODEL	
EQUATION	$15 - ? = 12$ $15 - 3 = 12$
PROBLEM	Marta had 10 stickers. She gave some away to her friend. Now she has 6 left. How many did she give away?
MODEL	
EQUATION	$10 - ? = 6$ $10 - 4 = 6$

TAKE FROM CHANGE UNKNOWN

1. Julie had 5 bananas. She gave some to Susie. Now she has 3. How many bananas did Julie give to Susie?

Way#1: Solve with a five frame

Way#2: Model with a number line

Way#3: Write a number sentence with a symbol for the part you don't know

_____-_____ = _____

TAKE FROM CHANGE UNKNOWN

2. Paul had 10 peaches. He ate some. Now he has 5. How many peaches did he eat?

Way#1: Solve with a ten frame

Way#2: Model with a number line

1 2 3 4 5 6 7 8 9 10 11 12 13 14 15 16 17 18 19 20

Way#3: Write a number sentence with a symbol for the part you don't know

_____ - _____ = _____

TAKE FROM CHANGE UNKNOWN

3. The bakery had 20 lemon cupcakes. They sold some and now they have 11 left. How many did they sell?

Way#1: Solve with a double ten frame.

Way#2: Model with a number line

1 2 3 4 5 6 7 8 9 10 11 12 13 14 15 16 17 18 19 20

Way#3: Write a number sentence with a symbol for the part you don't know

_____ - _____ = _____

TAKE FROM CHANGE UNKNOWN

4. The candy store had 12 lollipops. They sold some and now they have 3 left. How many did they sell?

Way#1: Solve with a drawing

Way#2: Model with a number line

<---- 1 2 3 4 5 6 7 8 9 10 11 12 13 14 15 16 17 18 19 20 ---->

Way#3: Write a number sentence with a symbol for the part you don't know

_____ - _____ = _____

TAKE FROM CHANGE UNKNOWN

5. The clothing store had 14 ties. They sold some and now they have 8. How many did they sell?

Way#1: Solve with a drawing

Way#2: Model with a number line

$$\longleftarrow \quad 1 \ 2 \ 3 \ 4 \ 5 \ 6 \ 7 \ 8 \ 9 \ 10 \ 11 \ 12 \ 13 \ 14 \ 15 \ 16 \ 17 \ 18 \ 19 \ 20 \quad \longrightarrow$$

Way#3: Write a number sentence with a symbol for the part you don't know

_____ - _____ = _____

TAKE FROM CHANGE UNKNOWN

6. Farmer Todd had 10 bunnies. He sold some bunnies. Now Farmer Todd has 2 bunnies left. How many bunnies did Farmer Todd sell?

Way#1: Model with a number bond

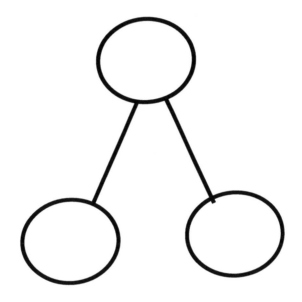

Way#2: Model with a number line

1 2 3 4 5 6 7 8 9 10 11 12 13 14 15 16 17 18 19 20

Way#3: Write a number sentence with a symbol for the part you don't know

_____ - _____ = _____

TAKE FROM CHANGE UNKNOWN

7. The deli had 20 bags of chips. They sold several during the day. They have 7 bags left. How many did they sell?

Way#1: Model with a number bond

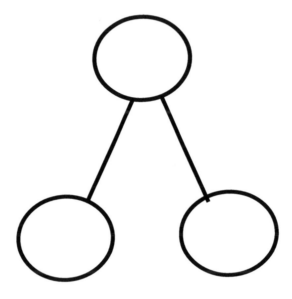

Way#2: Model with a number line

Way#3: Write a number sentence with a symbol for the part you don't know

_____ - _____ = _____

Problem Solving with Math Models© 2012

TAKE FROM CHANGE UNKNOWN

8. The candy store had 20 candy bars. They sold some. Now they have 1 left. How many did they sell?

Way#1: Solve with a double ten frame.

Way#2: Model with a number line

1 2 3 4 5 6 7 8 9 10 11 12 13 14 15 16 17 18 19 20

Way#3: Write a number sentence with a symbol for the part you don't know

_____ - _____ = _____

CHAPTER 2 QUIZ:
TAKE FROM CHANGE UNKNOWN PROBLEMS

Solve with a model:

1. Mason had 10 rocks. He gave some to his friend. Now he has 7. How many did he give to his friend?

2. Marta had 8 posters. She gave some away. Now she has 4. How many did she give away?

Problem Solving with Math Models© 2012

3. Roy had 16 toy trucks. He gave some away. Now he has 11 toy trucks. How many did he give away?

4. The jewelry store had 17 necklaces. They sold some of them. Now they have 5 left. How many did they sell?

UNIT 2 TEST:
TAKE FROM PROBLEMS

Solve with a model:

1. Matt had 10 coloring books. He gave away 2. How many does he have left?

2. Zack had 16 trading cards. He gave some away and now he has 8 left. How many did he give away?

Problem Solving with Math Models© 2012

3. Hong had 20 bicycles. He gave some away and now he has 14 left. How many did he give away?

4. Amanda had 19 stickers. She gave away 7 of them. How many does she have left?

CHAPTER 1
PUT TOGETHER/TAKE APART PROBLEMS

These types of problems are about sets of things. In them we know both parts and we are looking for the whole. What distinguishes a Put Together/Take Apart Problem from an Add to Result Unknown problem is action. In a Put together/Take Apart Problem there is no action only a set of something.

PROBLEM	Kiyana had five red apples and five green ones. How many apples did he have altogether?
MODEL	
EQUATION	5 + 5 = ? 5 + 5 = 10
PROBLEM	Marvin had 4 football trading cards and 6 baseball trading cards. How many cards did he have altogether?
MODEL (NUMBER LINE)	
EQUATION	4 + 6 = ? 4 + 6 = 10

PUT TOGETHER/TAKE APART—WHOLE UNKNOWN

1. Lucy has 3 gold rings and 2 silver rings. How many rings does she have altogether?

Way#1: Solve with a five frame

Way#2: Model with a number line

Way#3: Write a number sentence with a symbol for the part you don't know

_____+_____ = _____

PUT TOGETHER/TAKE APART—WHOLE UNKNOWN

2.   Grandma Betsy baked 5 lemon pies and then 3 chocolate pies. How many pies did she bake in all?

Way#1: Solve with a ten frame

Way#2: Model with a number line

1 2 3 4 5 6 7 8 9 10 11 12 13 14 15 16 17 18 19 20

Way#3: Write a number sentence with a symbol for the part you don't know

_____ + _____ = _____

Problem Solving with Math Models© 2012

PUT TOGETHER/TAKE APART—WHOLE UNKNOWN

3. Luke has 8 green marbles and 2 blue marbles. How many marbles does he have altogether?

Way#1: Solve with a ten frame

Way#2: Model with a number line

```
←————————————————————————————————————→
  1  2  3  4  5  6  7  8  9  10  11  12  13  14  15  16  17  18  19  20
```

Way#3: Write a number sentence with a symbol for the part you don't know

_____ + _____ = _____

PUT TOGETHER/TAKE APART—WHOLE UNKNOWN

4. There were 10 orange butterflies and 8 pink ones on the tree. How many butterflies were on the tree?

Way#1: Solve with a double ten frame.

Way#2: Model with a number line

1 2 3 4 5 6 7 8 9 10 11 12 13 14 15 16 17 18 19 20

Way#3: Write a number sentence with a symbol for the part you don't know

_____ + _____ = _____

Problem Solving with Math Models© 2012

PUT TOGETHER/TAKE APART—WHOLE UNKNOWN

5. There were 3 brown beetles, 5 orange beetles, and 4 black beetles on the tree. How many beetles were there altogether?

Way#1: Solve with a double ten frame.

Way#2: Model with a number line

1 2 3 4 5 6 7 8 9 10 11 12 13 14 15 16 17 18 19 20

Way#3: Write a number sentence with a symbol for the part you don't know

_____ + _____ = _____

Put Together/Take Apart—Whole Unknown

6.   There were 4 purple bicycles and 1 blue bicycle in the bicycle shop. How many bicycles were in the bicycle shop?

Way#1: Model with a number bond

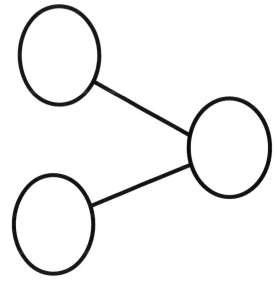

Way#2: Model with a number line

1 2 3 4 5 6 7 8 9 10 11 12 13 14 15 16 17 18 19 20

Way#3: Write a number sentence with a symbol for the part you don't know

_____+_____=_____

PUT TOGETHER/TAKE APART - WHOLE UNKNOWN

7.   There are 4 pink flowers and 5 yellow flowers in a vase. How many flowers were in the vase?

Way#1: Model with a number bond

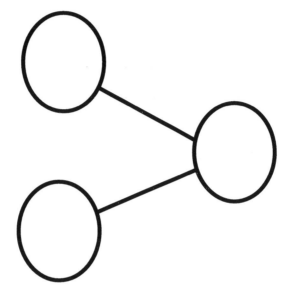

Way#2: Model with a number line

$\longleftrightarrow$
1 2 3 4 5 6 7 8 9 10 11 12 13 14 15 16 17 18 19 20

Way#3: Write a number sentence with a symbol for the part you don't know

_____+_____=_____

PUT TOGETHER/TAKE APART—WHOLE UNKNOWN

8.   The toy store had 10 toy cars and 10 toy trucks. How many toy vehicles did they have altogether?

Way#1: Model with a number bond

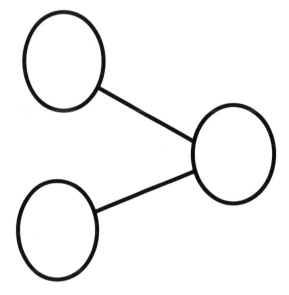

Way#2: Model with a number line

1 2 3 4 5 6 7 8 9 10 11 12 13 14 15 16 17 18 19 20

Way#3: Write a number sentence with a symbol for the part you don't know

_____ + _____ = _____

CHAPTER 1 QUIZ:
PUT TOGETHER/ TAKE APART - WHOLE UNKNOWN PROBLEMS

Solve with a model:

1. The bakery had 2 strawberry cakes and 2 lemon ones. How many cakes did they have altogether?

2. Mike had 7 blue shirts and 3 black ones in a bag. How many shirts did he have in the bag?

3. The pizza shop baked 9 pepperoni pizzas and 8 cheese pizzas. How many pizzas did they bake?

4. The fruit stand had 7 bags of apples, 8 bags of oranges, and 5 bags of bananas. How many bags of fruit did they have altogether?

CHAPTER 2
PUT TOGETHER/ TAKE APART– BOTH ADDENDS UNKNOWN

These types of problems are Put Together/Take Apart problems with both addends unknown. In these problems we are talking about sets of something. In this particular type of problem we are talking about all the ways a set can be put together. For example, we have 4 markers. Some are green and some are yellow. How many could be green and how many could be yellow? We could have 3 green and 1 yellow, 2 green and 2 yellow or 1 green and 3 yellow. Students have to find all the ways to do that problem.

With this type of problem we could model our thinking by using real objects, pictures, diagrams, or tables. When you have your students use concrete materials, they can see what is happening. When you have the students solve it with pictures they learn how to organize information and draw it out. Then, when they use a table, they are working at an abstract level.

You want to emphasize that it is important to organize information in a way that other people can tell what you did. It is important to show our work. It is important to be neat.

TRY DRAWING PICTURES TO HELP!

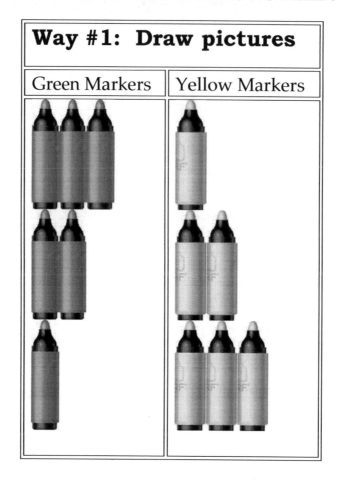

Way #2: Using The Table Technique.

MARKERS	
GREEN	YELLOW
3	1
2	2
1	3

Problem Solving with Math Models© 2012

PUT TOGETHER/TAKE APART--BOTH ADDENDS UNKNOWN

1. There are some children on the swings at the park. There are 5 children in all. How many could be girls? How many could be boys? There are some boys and some girls.

Way#1: Draw pictures

Way#2: Solve with a table

STUDENTS IN CLASS	
GIRLS	BOYS
4	1
3	
2	
1	

PUT TOGETHER/TAKE APART--BOTH ADDENDS UNKNOWN

2. Raul has 6 kites. Some are blue and some are purple. How many of each could he have? There are some of each.

Way#1: Draw pictures

Way#2: Solve with a table

KITES	
BLUE	PURPLE
5	1
4	
3	
2	
1	

PUT TOGETHER/TAKE APART--BOTH ADDENDS UNKNOWN

3.   There are 7 slices of pizza. Some are pepperoni and some are cheese. How many of each could there be? There are some of each.

Way#1: Draw pictures

Way#2: Solve with a table

PIZZA	
PEPPERONI	**CHEESE**
6	1
5	
4	
3	
2	
1	

PUT TOGETHER/TAKE APART--BOTH ADDENDS UNKNOWN

4. The pet store has some dogs and some cats. There are 8 animals in total. How many dogs could there be? How many cats could there be? There are some of each.

Way#1: Draw pictures

Way#2: Solve with a table

PETS	
DOGS	CATS
7	1
6	
5	
4	
3	
2	
1	

PUT TOGETHER/TAKE APART--BOTH ADDENDS UNKNOWN

5. The aquarium has some fish. There are 9 in all. Some are big and some are small. How many big fish could there be? How many small fish could there be? There were some of each.

Way#1: Draw pictures

Way#2: Solve with a table

FISH	
BIG	SMALL
8	
7	
6	
5	
4	
3	
2	
1	

CHAPTER 2 QUIZ:
PUT TOGETHER/TAKE APART - BOTH ADDENDS UNKNOWN

Solve with a model:

1. Jake had 4 cookies. Some were chocolate and some were vanilla. How many of each could he have had?

2. Brett had 5 toy vehicles. Some were trucks and some were cars. How many of each could he have had?

3. Megan had 7 candies. Some of them were lemon and some were strawberry. How many of each could she have had?

4. Sara had 8 rings. Some were gold and some were silver. How many of each could she have had?

CHAPTER 3
PUT TOGETHER/TAKE APART PROBLEMS PART UNKNOWN

These types of problems are about sets of things. In them we know the total and one part of the set. We are looking for the other part of the set.

PROBLEM	Hong had ten apples. Five were red apples and the rest were green. How many apples were green?
MODEL	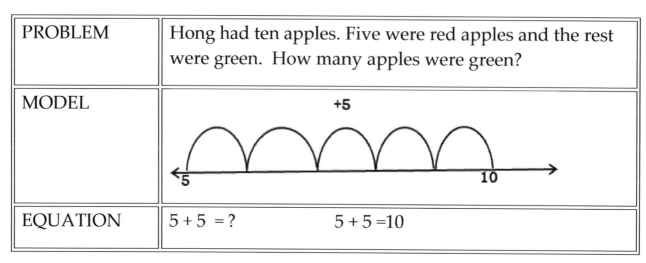
EQUATION	5 + 5 = ? 5 + 5 =10

PROBLEM	Grace had 15 lollipops. Ten were red and the rest were yellow. How many were yellow?
MODEL	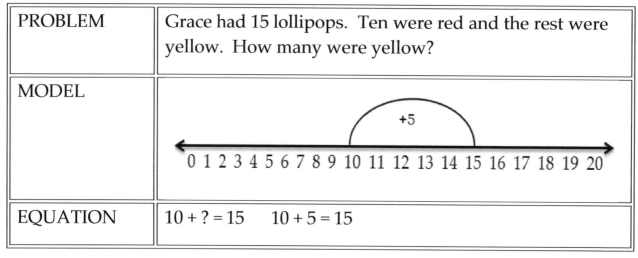
EQUATION	10 + ? = 15 10 + 5 = 15

Put Together/Take Apart - Part Unknown

1. Kate had 5 pogo sticks. Three were blue and the rest were green. How many were green?

Way#1: Solve with a ten frame

<table>
<tr><td></td><td></td><td></td><td></td><td></td></tr>
<tr><td></td><td></td><td></td><td></td><td></td></tr>
</table>

Way#2: Model with a number line

1 2 3 4 5 6 7 8 9 10 11 12 13 14 15 16 17 18 19 20

Way#3: Write a number sentence with a symbol for the part you don't know

_____ + _____ = _____

PUT TOGETHER/TAKE APART - PART UNKNOWN

2. Leo had 10 toy vehicles. Seven were trucks and the rest were cars. How many were cars?

Way#1: Solve with a double ten frame.

Way#2: Model with a number line

1 2 3 4 5 6 7 8 9 10 11 12 13 14 15 16 17 18 19 20

Way#3: Write a number sentence with a symbol for the part you don't know

_____ + _____ = _____

Put Together/Take Apart - Part Unknown

3. Farmer John had 12 apples. Six were red and the rest were green. How many were green?

Way#1: Solve with a double ten frame.

Way#2: Model with a number line

1 2 3 4 5 6 7 8 9 10 11 12 13 14 15 16 17 18 19 20

Way#3: Write a number sentence with a symbol for the part you don't know

_____ + _____ = _____

Put Together/Take Apart - Part Unknown

4.   The pet store had 14 animals. Nine were dogs and the rest were cats. How many were cats?

Way#1: Solve with a double ten frame.

Way#2: Model with a number line

1 2 3 4 5 6 7 8 9 10 11 12 13 14 15 16 17 18 19 20

Way#3: Write a number sentence with a symbol for the part you don't know

_____ + _____ = _____

PUT TOGETHER/TAKE APART - PART UNKNOWN

5. Farmer Joe had 12 cows on his farm. Some were white and some were brown. Eight were white. How many were brown?

Way#1: Model with a number bond

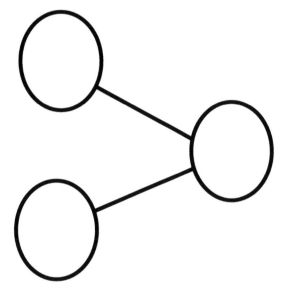

Way#2: Model with a number line

Way#3: Write a number sentence with a symbol for the part you don't know

_____ + _____ = _____

PUT TOGETHER/TAKE APART - PART UNKNOWN

6. The pizza shop had 12 slices of pizza. Nine were pepperoni. The rest were cheese. How many were cheese?

Way#1: Model with a number bond

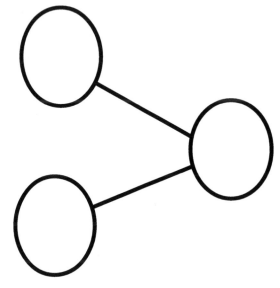

Way#2: Model with a number line

1 2 3 4 5 6 7 8 9 10 11 12 13 14 15 16 17 18 19 20

Way#3: Write a number sentence with a symbol for the part you don't know

_____ + _____ = _____

PUT TOGETHER/TAKE APART—PART UNKNOWN

7. The deli had 17 sandwiches. Nine were turkey and the rest were chicken. How many were chicken?

Way#1: Model with a number bond

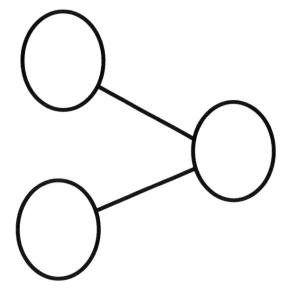

Way#2: Model with a number line

1 2 3 4 5 6 7 8 9 10 11 12 13 14 15 16 17 18 19 20

Way#3: Write a number sentence with a symbol for the part you don't know

_____ + _____ = _____

PUT TOGETHER/TAKE APART - PART UNKNOWN

8.   The pet store had 15 fish. Fourteen were goldfish and the rest were rainbow fish. How many were rainbow fish?

Way#1: Solve with a double ten frame.

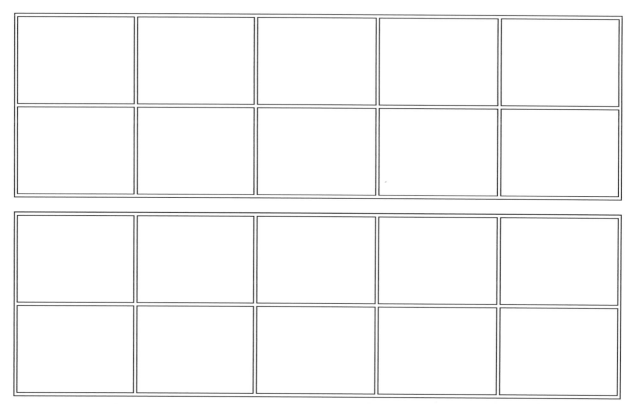

Way#2: Model with a number line

1 2 3 4 5 6 7 8 9 10 11 12 13 14 15 16 17 18 19 20

Way#3: Write a number sentence with a symbol for the part you don't know

_____ + _____ = _____

CHAPTER 3 QUIZ:
PUT TOGETHER/TAKE APART - PART UNKNOWN

Solve with a model:

1. The fruit stand had 5 apples. Four were red and the rest were green. How many were green?

2. Hong had 10 marbles. Eight were orange and the rest were blue. How many were blue?

3.   Marvin had 15 trading cards. Ten were soccer cards and the rest were baseball cards. How many baseball cards did he have?

4.   The bakery had 12 cookies. Five were lemon and the rest were chocolate. How many were chocolate?

CHAPTER 1
COMPARE DIFFERENCE UNKNOWN

In these problems students are comparing two or more amounts. They are comparing to find out what is the difference between the amounts. There are two versions of this type of story. One version uses the word more and one version uses the word fewer. The version with the word fewer is more difficult.

PROBLEM MORE VERSION	John had 12 marbles. Carl had 2 marbles. How many more marbles does John have than Carl?
MODEL	John Difference is 10 Carl 2 12
EQUATION	2 + ? = 12 2 + 10 = 12
PROBLEM FEWER VERSION	Carl had 2 marbles. John had 12 marbles. How many fewer marbles did Carl have than John?
MODEL	John Carl
EQUATION	2 + ? = 12 2 + 10 = 12

COMPARE DIFFERENCE UNKNOWN

1. John had 5 grapes. Mike had 3. How many more grapes did John have than Mike?

Way#1: Solve with pictures

Way#2: Solve with numbers

Explain your thinking:

Problem Solving with Math Models© 2012

COMPARE DIFFERENCE UNKNOWN

2.   Kelly had 5 bracelets. Sue had 9 bracelets. How many more bracelets did Sue have than Kelly?

Way#1: Solve with pictures

Way#2: Solve with numbers

Explain your thinking:

COMPARE DIFFERENCE UNKNOWN

3. The bakery had 8 vanilla bars and 10 lemon ones. How many more lemon bars did it have than vanilla ones?

Way#1: Solve with pictures

Way#2: Solve with numbers

Explain your thinking:

COMPARE DIFFERENCE UNKNOWN

4. Tiffany had 5 necklaces and Maria had 2. How many fewer necklaces did Maria have than Marta?

Way#1: Solve with pictures

Way#2: Solve with numbers

Explain your thinking:

COMPARE DIFFERENCE UNKNOWN

5. The candy store had 7 grape lollipops and 8 cherry ones. How many fewer grape lollipops did it have than cherry ones?

Way#1: Solve with pictures

Way#2: Solve with numbers

Explain your thinking:

COMPARE DIFFERENCE UNKNOWN

6. Jamal had 8 soccer trading cards and 3 baseball ones. How many fewer baseball ones did he have than soccer ones?

Way#1: Solve with a double number line

Way#2: Solve with numbers

Explain your thinking:

COMPARE DIFFERENCE UNKNOWN

7. The bakery had 18 lemon cupcakes and 12 strawberry ones. How many fewer strawberry ones did it have than lemon ones?

Way#1: Solve with a double number line

Way#2: Solve with numbers

Explain your thinking:

COMPARE DIFFERENCE UNKNOWN

8.   Derek had 20 blue marbles and 10 green ones. How many more blue marbles did he have than green ones?

Way#1: Solve with a double number line

Way#2: Solve with numbers

Explain your thinking:

CHAPTER 1 QUIZ:
COMPARE DIFFERENCE UNKNOWN PROBLEMS

Solve with a model:

1. Amanda had 5 gold rings and 3 black rings. How many more gold rings did she have than black ones?

2. Jamal had 10 baseball trading cards and 2 basketball ones. How many more baseball cards did he have than basketball ones?

 Problem Solving with Math Models© 2012

3.   The bakery had 17 chocolate candies and 4 lemon ones. How many fewer lemon candies did it have than chocolate ones?

4.   Grandma decorated 10 cupcakes with strawberry frosting and 5 with lemon. How many fewer cupcakes had lemon frosting than strawberry?

CHAPTER 2
COMPARISON – BIGGER PART UNKNOWN

In these problems students are comparing two or more amounts. They are comparing to find out who had the bigger part. There are two versions of this type of story. One version uses the word more and one version uses the word fewer. The version with the word fewer is more difficult.

PROBLEM MORE VERSION	Lucy has 5 more marbles than Carl. Carl has 2 marbles. How many marbles does Lucy have?
MODEL	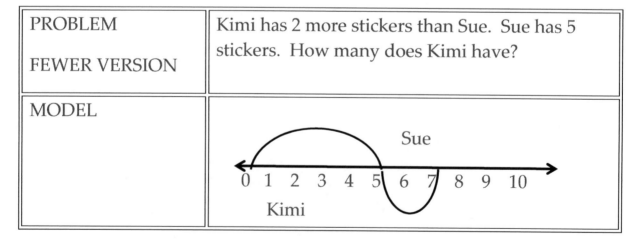
EQUATION	$2 + 5 = ?$ $\qquad$ $2 + 5 = 7$

PROBLEM FEWER VERSION	Kimi has 2 more stickers than Sue. Sue has 5 stickers. How many does Kimi have?
MODEL	

COMPARISON – BIGGER PART UNKNOWN

1. Daniel has 9 comic books. Nathan has 11 more than he does. How many comic books does Nathan have?

Way#1: Solve with pictures

Way#2: Solve with numbers

Explain your thinking:

COMPARISON – BIGGER PART UNKNOWN

2. Mike has 4 toy airplanes. Joshua has 4 more toy airplanes than Mike. How many toy airplanes does Joshua have?

Way#1: Solve with pictures

Way#2: Solve with numbers

Explain your thinking:

COMPARISON – BIGGER PART UNKNOWN

3. Erica has 7 earrings. Sue has 3 more than that. How many earrings does Sue have?

Way #1: Solve with pictures

Way #2: Solve with numbers

Explain your thinking:

COMPARISON – BIGGER PART UNKNOWN

4. Maria has 7 dolls. Macy has 7 more than that. How many dolls does Macy have?

Way#1: Solve with pictures

Way#2: Solve with numbers

Explain your thinking:

Problem Solving with Math Models© 2012

COMPARISON – BIGGER PART UNKNOWN

5. Carol has 8 candy bars. Grace has 2 more than Carol. How many candy bars does Grace have?

Way#1: Solve with a double number line

Way#2: Solve with numbers

Explain your thinking:

COMPARISON – BIGGER PART UNKNOWN

6. Lisa has 10 hair brushes. Kimmy has 8 more marbles than Lisa. How many hair brushes does Kimmy have?

Way#1: Solve with a double number line

Way#2: Solve with numbers

Explain your thinking:

Problem Solving with Math Models© 2012

Comparison – Bigger Part Unknown

7. Farmer John has 15 brown rabbits. He has 5 more black rabbits than brown ones. How many black rabbits does Farmer John have?

Way#1: Solve with a double number line

Way#2: Solve with numbers

Explain your thinking:

COMPARISON – BIGGER PART UNKNOWN

8. The zoo has 5 lions. It has 2 more bears than lions. How many bears does the zoo have?

Way#1: Solve with a double number line

Way#2: Solve with numbers

Explain your thinking:

Problem Solving with Math Models© 2012

CHAPTER 2 QUIZ:
COMPARE BIGGER PART UNKNOWN

Solve with a model:

1. Jake had 3 pieces of gum. Clark had 4 more pieces than Jake. How many pieces of gum did Clark have?

2. Linda had 7 rings. Sue had 7 more rings than Linda. How many rings did Sue have?

3. The candy store had 12 cherry lollipops. It had 4 more lemon ones than cherry ones. How many lemon lollipops did it have?

4. The store made 12 banana shakes. It made 5 more chocolate shakes than banana ones. How many chocolate shakes did it make?

CHAPTER 3
COMPARISON – SMALLER PART UNKNOWN

$\mathbf{I}$n these problems students are comparing two or more amounts. They are comparing to find out who has the smaller amount. There are two versions of this type of story. One version uses the word more and one version uses the word fewer. The version with the word fewer is more difficult.

PROBLEM MORE VERSION	John had 5 marbles. Carl had 4 fewer marbles than he did. How many marbles does Carl have?
MODEL	John ⬤ ⬤ ⬤ ⬤⬤ Carl ⬤
EQUATION	$5 - 4 = ?$ $5 - 4 = 1$

PROBLEM FEWER VERSION	Carl had 10 fewer marbles than John. John had 12 marbles. How many marbles did Carl have?
MODEL	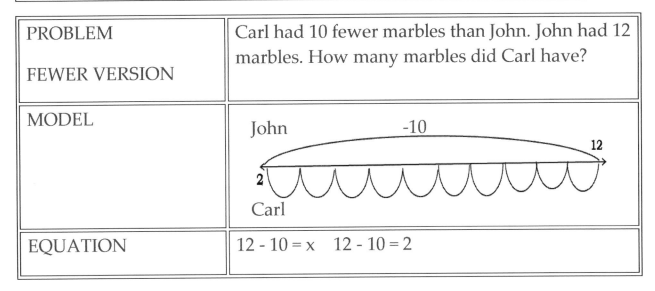
EQUATION	$12 - 10 = x$ $12 - 10 = 2$

COMPARISON – SMALLER PART UNKNOWN

1. Tom had 5 marbles. Ken had 4 fewer marbles than Tom. How many marbles did Ken have?

Way#1: Solve with pictures

Way#2: Solve with numbers

Explain your thinking:

COMPARISON – SMALLER PART UNKNOWN

2. Ann had 7 rings. June had 4 fewer rings. How many
    rings did June have?

Way#1: Solve with pictures

Way#2: Solve with numbers

Explain your thinking:

COMPARISON – SMALLER PART UNKNOWN

3. Jake had 8 trading cards. Mike had 4 fewer trading cards than he did. How many trading cards did Mike have?

Way#1: Solve with pictures

Way#2: Solve with numbers

Explain your thinking:

Problem Solving with Math Models© 2012

COMPARISON – SMALLER PART UNKNOWN

4. There are 12 pink butterflies. There are 8 fewer orange ones. How many orange ones are there?

Way#1: Solve with pictures

Way#2: Solve with numbers

Explain your thinking:

COMPARISON – SMALLER PART UNKNOWN

5. Luke has 14 toy trucks. He has 2 fewer toy cars. How many toy cars does he have?

Way#1: Solve with a double number line

Way#2: Solve with numbers

Explain your thinking:

COMPARISON – SMALLER PART UNKNOWN

6. The bakery made 12 chocolate chip cookies. It made 3 fewer lemon ones than chocolate chip ones. How many lemon cookies did it make?

Way#1: Solve with a double number line

Way#2: Solve with numbers

Explain your thinking:

COMPARISON – SMALLER PART UNKNOWN

7. The pizza shop had 20 slices of pepperoni pizza. It had 2 fewer veggie slices than pepperoni slices. How many veggie slices did it have?

Way#1: Solve with a double number line

Way#2: Solve with numbers

Explain your thinking:

COMPARISON – SMALLER PART UNKNOWN

8. The jewelry store had 20 silver rings. It had 12 fewer gold rings. How many gold rings did it have?

Way#1: Solve with an open number line

Way#2: Solve with numbers

Explain your thinking:

CHAPTER 3 QUIZ:
COMPARE SMALLER UNKNOWN PROBLEMS

Solve with a model:

1. Grace had 10 scarves. Linda had 5 fewer scarves than Grace. How many scarves did Linda have?

2. Hong had 12 soccer balls. Luke had 2 fewer than that. How many soccer balls did Luke have?

3. Trevor had 15 toy helicopters. Larry had 6 fewer than Trevor. How many toy helicopters did Larry have?

4. The bakery had 20 cherry cupcakes. It had 7 fewer lemon cupcakes than cherry ones. How many lemon cupcakes did it have?

Unit 4 Test:
Compare Problems

Solve with a model:

1. Luke had 15 board games. John had 8 board games. How many more games did Luke have than John?

2. Jackie had 10 hats. Sharon had 20 hats. How many fewer hats did Jackie have than Sharon?

Problem Solving with Math Models© 2012

3. John had 2 candies. Mike had 6 more than John did. How many candies did Mike have?

4. Kelly had 12 bracelets. Macy had 7 fewer bracelets than Kelly. How many bracelets did Macy have?

5. Raul had 4 toy trucks. For his birthday he got 5 more from his brother, 3 from his sister, and 7 from his grandmother. How many toy trucks does he have now?

NAME:

DATE:

Solve the problems. Show your thinking by drawing a picture, using a number line, or making a table.

1. Carl had 5 dollars. His grandmother gave him 5 more. How many dollars does he have now?

2. Luke had 9 gumballs. His brother gave him some more. Now he has 17 gumballs. How many did his brother give him?

Problem Solving with Math Models© 2012

3. Mary had 20 coats. She gave 5 to her sister. How many does she have now?

4. Ricky had 15 toy robots. He gave some to his cousin. Now he has 8. How many did he give to his cousin?

5. Maria had 7 hair bows. Carol had 5 hair bows. How many more hair bows did Maria have than Carol?

6. Larry had 10 crayons. John had 12 crayons. How many fewer crayons did Larry have than John?

7. Linda had 5 dolls. Sharon had 2 more dolls than Linda did. How many dolls did Sharon have?

8. Marvin had 10 toy dump trucks. Tim had 2 fewer toy trucks than that. How many toy dump trucks did Tim have?

9. The bakery made 14 cakes. Eleven were chocolate and the rest were vanilla. How many were vanilla?

10. There are 7 humming birds on a flower. Some are orange and some are blue. How many could there be of each color?

11. The fruit stand has 9 red apples and 8 green ones. How many apples do they have altogether?

Unit 1
Add to Problems

Chapter 1: Add to Result Unknown Problems
1. 5 marbles
2. 5 baseballs
3. 5 flowers
4. 6 rocks
5. 10 action figures
6. 10 pennies
7. 20 cupcakes
8. 12 fruits

Chapter 1 Quiz: Add to Result Unknown
1. 7 marbles
2. 14 rings
3. 14 action figures
4. 9 bracelets

Chapter 2: Add to Change Unknown Problems
1. 2 toy airplanes
2. 2 cookies
3. 7 toy soldiers
4. 6 toy cars
5. 7 stuffed animals
6. 5 seashells
7. 5 cookies
8. 8 action figures

Chapter 2 Quiz: Add to Change Unknown Problem
1. 4 stickers
2. 5 marbles
3. 8 cookies
4. 9 pizzas

Unit 1 Test: Addition Problems
1. 3 dress
2. 11 basketballs
3. 15 pies
4. 1 seashells

Unit 2
Take From Problems

Chapter 1: Take From Result Unknown
1. 3 apples
2. 5 stickers
3. 6 marbles
4. 6 stamps
5. 2 books
6. 7 stickers
7. 10 baseballs
8. 7 peaches

Chapter 1 Quiz: Take From Result Unknown Problems
1. 8 kittens
2. 5 seashells
3. 4 toy cars
4. 9 brownies

Chapter 2: Take From Change Unknown Problems
1. 2 bananas
2. 5 peaches
3. 9 cupcakes
4. 9 lollipops
5. 6 ties
6. 8 bunnies
7. 13 bags
8. 19 candy bars

Chapter 2 Quiz: Take From Change
Unknown Problems
1. 3 rocks
2. 4 posters
3. 5 toy trucks
4. 12 necklaces

UNIT 2 TEST: Take From Problems
1. 8 coloring books
2. 8 trading cards
3. 6 bicycles
4. 12 stickers

UNIT 3
PUT TOGETHER/TAKE APART
PROBLEMS

Chapter 1: Put Together/Take Apart—Whole Unknown Problems
1. 5 rings
2. 8 pies
3. 10 marbles
4. 18 butterflies
5. 12 beetles
6. 5 bicycles
7. 9 flowers
8. 20 toy vehicles

Chapter 1 Quiz: Put Together/Take Apart—Whole Unknown Problems
1. 4 cakes
2. 10 shirts
3. 17 pizzas
4. 20 bags

Chapter 2: Put Together/Take Apart—Both Addends Unknown

1. Students In Class	
Girls	Boys
4	1
3	2
2	3
1	4

2. Marbles	
Blue	Purple
5	1
4	2
3	3
2	4
1	5

3. Slices of Pizza	
Pepperoni	Cheese
6	1
5	2
4	3
3	4
2	5
1	6

4. Pets	
Dogs	Cats
7	1
6	2
5	3
4	4
3	5
2	6
1	7

5. Fish	
Big	Small
8	1
7	2
6	3
5	4
4	5
3	6
2	7
1	8

Chapter 2 Quiz: Put Together/Take Apart—Both Addends Unknown

1. Cookies	
Chocolate	Vanilla
3	1
2	2
1	3

2. Toy Vehicles	
Trucks	Cars
4	1
3	2
2	3
1	4

3. Candies	
Lemon	Strawberry
6	1
5	2
4	3
3	4
2	5
1	6

4. Rings	
Gold	Silver
7	1
6	2
5	3
4	4
3	5
2	6
1	7

Chapter 3: Put Together/Take Apart—Part Unknown Problems

1. 2 green pogo sticks
2. 3 toy cars
3. 6 green apples
4. 5 cats
5. 4 brown cows
6. 3 cheese slices
7. 8 chicken sandwiches
8. 1 rainbow fish

Chapter 3 Quiz: Put Together/Take Apart—Part Unknown Problems

1. 1 green apple
2. 2 blue marbles
3. 5 baseball cards
4. 7 chocolate cookies

Problem Solving with Math Models© 2012

Unit 4
Comparison—Difference Unknown Problems

Chapter 1: Compare Difference Unknown Problems
1. 2 more grapes
2. 4 more bracelets
3. 2 more lemon bars
4. 3 fewer necklaces
5. 1 fewer grape lollipops
6. 5 fewer baseball cards
7. 6 fewer strawberry ones
8. 10 more blue marbles

Chapter 1 Quiz: Compare Difference Unknown Problems
1. 2 more gold rings
2. 8 more baseball cards
3. 13 fewer lemon candies
4. 5 fewer lemon cupcakes

Chapter 2: Compare—Bigger Part Unknown Problems
1. 20 comic books
2. 8 toy airplanes
3. 10 earrings
4. 14 dolls
5. 10 candy bars
6. 18 hair brushes
7. 20 black rabbits
8. 7 bears

Chapter 2 Quiz: Compare—Bigger Part Unknown Problems
1. 7 pieces of gum
2. 14 rings
3. 16 lemon lollipops
4. 17 chocolate shakes

Chapter 3: Comparison—Smaller Part Unknown Problems
1. 1 marble
2. 3 rings
3. 4 trading cards
4. 4 orange butterflies
5. 12 toy cars
6. 9 lemon cookies
7. 18 veggie slices
8. 8 gold rings

Chapter 3 Quiz: Comparison Smaller Unknown Problems
1. 5 scarves
2. 10 soccer balls
3. 9 toy helicopters
4. 13 lemon cupcakes

UNIT 4 TEST: Compare Problems
1. 7 more board games
2. 10 fewer hats
3. 8 candies
4. 5 bracelets
5. 19 toy trucks

FINAL WORD PROBLEM TEST

1. 10 dollars
2. 8 gumballs
3. 15 hats
4. 7 toy robots
5. 2 more hair bows
6. 2 fewer crayons
7. 7 dolls
8. 8 toy dumb trucks
9. 3 vanilla cupcakes

10. Humming Birds	
Orange	Blue
6	1
5	2
4	3
3	4
2	5
1	6

11. 17 apples

Problem Solving with Math Models© 2012

REFERENCES

Carpenter, T., Fennema, E., Franke, M., Levi, L., & Empson, S. (1999). *Children's Mathematics: Cognitively Guided Instruction*. Portsmouth, NH: Heinemann.

Common Core Standards Writing Team (Bill McCullum, lead author). (2011, June 20). *Progressions for the common core state standards in mathematics: K-3, Categorical data; Grades 2-5, Measurement Data (draft)*. Retrieved from: www.commoncoretools.wordpress.com.

Common Core Standards Writing Team (Bill McCullum, lead author). (2011, May 29). *Progressions for the common core state standards in mathematics: K, Counting and cardinality; K-5, operations and algebraic thinking (draft)*. Retrieved from www.commoncoretools.wordpress.com.

Peterson, P. L., Carpenter, T. P., & Loef, M. (1989). *Teachers' Pedagogical Content Beliefs in Mathematics. Cognition and Instruction*, Vol. 6, No. 1, pp. 1-40.

Made in the USA
Charleston, SC
30 May 2015